(A book for the lonely, frustrated Nashville songwriter by someone who's been there)

Liz Hengber

Cold Tree Press
Nashville, Tennessee

Published by Cold Tree Press
Nashville, Tennessee
www.coldtreepress.com

Printed in the United States of America
ISBN 1-58385-107-0

To my father Jack Hengber
who moved me down to Nashville in 1986
in his '73 Oldsmobile Cutlass Supreme...
Thanks for the car, the belief
and your unconditional love.

Author's Note

I wrote this book with the assumption that you have come to Nashville with the intention of landing a writing deal. It's the only frame of reference I have. My writing deal lead to my success as a writer and I feel strongly that it might never have happened without my company behind me. However, this is just my experience. There are writers who have made it on their own without a publisher...but that's not my story. Hopefully my experience can help you out.

A special thank you to Phil Foster and Terry Moran for putting their love and time into this book. It couldn't have gotten off the ground without you.

Introduction

When I first moved to Nashville in 1986 I was lonely, frustrated, confused and an absolute mess. I had no idea where to begin my pursuit as a songwriter. Every time I talked to a songwriter about their success, it just sounded like they were born into the business. Like they came to Nashville and in a week "Voila!!" Here's your writing deal. I was looking for answers. How do you get a company to sign you? How much should I spend on demos? Were you ever this confused?? None of these questions were answered. Instead I got "Things are so great for me!!!" So, alas, I was left to make mistakes and figure it out by myself. Five years later…Five long and frustrating years later, I finally landed a writing deal.

I swore to myself back then (back when nobody wanted me in their offices) that if I ever found a break in this business, I would share my knowledge. I want this book to be the light that I was searching for. There are no clear cut answers to anything in this business and everybody's luck is different. But a guide line is essential when you're a lost lonely and unrecognized songwriter in Nashville. To everybody that has purchased this book…These are the steps I took to making it in this business. There are other ways to make it… other opinions…but this is how it finally worked for me.

(A book for the lonely, frustrated
Nashville songwriter
by someone who's been there)

Part 1:

The Road to a Writing Deal

CHAPTER ONE

You've just arrived!

You've just arrived!

The best way for me to start this book is to share with you some of my early mistakes. And believe me, I made a ton of them. So here goes:

My first mistake... I was in a rush. I decided the minute I got to Nashville that I would give it one year to get a writing deal...I'm lying...I thought I could get one in 6 months. This not only didn't help my writing, it made me seem desperate. Big mistake. No one wants anything to do with you when you're desperate.

People tried to tell me to relax a little; that my anxiety to get things going was a little off putting to some. But I paid no attention. I kept demos in my pockets and gave them out to whoever would listen. I cornered successful songwriters at cafés and asked them to co-write. I was a walking example of what not to do. And the funny thing is, I wasn't even writing that much. I just concentrated on getting what I came to town with recorded. No one could tell me they weren't even remotely commercial country songs. I wouldn't listen to that nonsense. Instead I was on a mission, and advice was something I had no time for. I wonder what would have happened if I had taken all that crazy energy I had and put it into writing great songs instead. Anyway, being in such a rush led me to...

My next mistake... going to visit publishers before I was ready. I can't even begin to tell you what a terrible mistake that was. Somewhere buried in the back of my mind, behind all my denial, I knew my songs weren't great yet. But did that stop me from making appointments with important Publishers?? Not

Me...no way...I walked right in there with my mediocre songs. Let me tell ya something guys...Publishers will meet with you once, but after that, if they don't like what they hear, they are going to be "out to Lunch" or "In a meeting" for life. I had become what is known as a *squirrel!*

Definition of a squirrel...any variety of rodent with a strong bushy tail and strong hind legs—or...*an annoying songwriter wanna be.* And what's worse is I really believed these guys were "Out to Lunch" at 4 in the afternoon. (Actually with some publishers, that might be true.)

My depression at never having my phone calls returned lead me sailing right into...

A very big mistake!!! I ended up hanging out in bars with what I call Black Holes...or *BITTER SONGWRITERS.* Six months in Nashville and I had already become road hard and hung out to dry. I was hanging with people that would spout "Ahhh it's all politics!" or "What do they know anyway" or even better "That song sucks!" After a couple of months of this, I sobered up pretty quickly. The last thing I wanted was to become one of these guys:

Your job: or,
"You want that on wheat or rye?"

Let's see...we're up to...errrr...it would be...

Yet another big mistake!!! My first six months in town I worked a full time 9 to 5 Job. I was a secretary. It was the kind of job you take home with you at night and that left me absolutely no time to be creative. The correct word for this kind of job is a *TRAP.* The better you are at it—the further you move away from song writing. Luckily I sucked as a secretary. I was fired after six months.

This left me to go back to the stereotypical job that unemployed show business people go into...WAITING TABLES. I did this at various different restaurants for 5 years until I was signed as a staff writer. Five long years of "Would you like cheese with that?" I hated it. But hating it is precisely the point. Hating it kept me hungry to make it as a writer. It also freed my days up. The business of music cannot just be done on a lunch hour or a day off. It happens from 9 to 5 like most jobs. You have to be available.

Back in those days I lived pretty simply...no car payments, cheap rent, Salvation Army furniture and absolutely no credit cards. I didn't want to acquire much because that would mean having to get a "REAL JOB" to pay for it all. Time and time again I see writers who move here and suddenly lose sight of the goal. They buy the new house and the new car and before you know it, they can't afford to try and break into the business.

Anyway, waiting tables worked for me. It may not necessarily work for you, but what ever job you find, make sure it's flexible. Make sure if you have a meeting at 10:30 on music row, you can show up without getting fired.

So my advice to you is:

1. What ever job you take, make sure it allows you the time to do business on Music Row.

2. Work a job that you leave behind when the shift is through. Your mind must be clear to write.

3. Don't lose sight of why you moved here. It wasn't to get a full time job that would take you further from your dreams.

CHAPTER THREE

Act like a staff writer, even if you're not.

Act like a staff writer, even if you're not.

So let's see. Two years have magically gone by now...I'm still waiting tables, writing fantastic songs every day, visiting publishers whenever I can, and basically working as hard as I can toward a staff writing deal...NOT! Oh I was still waiting tables...but what I was doing in my off time was far from music. This was *PARTY GIRL MISTAKE!!* Party girl mistake is a whole other book...not worth mentioning. Let's just say, I won't be running for a public office anytime soon—too many skeletons in the closet.

Anyway...one day I woke up. And on that day I decided to get my act together. I wanted more than anything to be a professional songwriter. *So it was time to act like one.* So everyday I would section off my writing time...usually between 9 and 2 in the afternoon. If I felt uninspired that day—I'd still try. Maybe brush up an old song that needed work. But regardless—this was my time to write. If a friend wanted me to go to the movies or the mall—I said no. Not during writing time. It was time to start pretending I was on staff already. It was the only way I would ever build up a catalogue.

At this point I also knew I was ready to start asking people to co-write with me. People who were on staff already. But I also knew I couldn't just do this without a plan. I was still a nobody trying to prove to everyone that I had talent. So I made copies of my demo's (which is something I will cover in the next chapter). I put three of my best songs on there. When I asked someone to write with me, I'd say "Listen to this and if you feel you like what I do, I'd love the chance to work with you." Out of every ten writers I asked to co-write, maybe two said yes. Terrible odds...but those two songs usually turned out pretty good.

When I entered a room with a writer, I made sure I came to the appointment prepared. I never expected them to have the idea...

they were good enough to write with someone who didn't have a deal, the least I could do was to come to the table with solid ideas. It was the only way I could get an appointment to write with them again. Not to mention I was also trying to impress their publisher... possibly get a deal there myself.

But let me stress that writing with someone on staff is not the only way to go. I wrote some amazing songs with people who were in the same boat as me.* And the writing appointments were a lot more relaxing! You just need to respect what they do.

So... What do you do if you don't have deal yet???

1. Start acting like a professional songwriter. Section off 4 or 5 hours to write everyday and be disciplined about it.

2. Start asking people you respect to co-write...don't be crushed if they say no. If you act like a professional, someday they'll say yes.

3. Be prepared for the appointment...come in with great ideas. Don't rely on your co-writer for this...not in the beginning. Remember, you're not only trying to impress them. You're trying to impress the publisher as well.

4. Stay FOCUSED!

If you pretend you're someone who does this for a living...there's a good chance you'll make it a reality.

** Ironically, my first cut was co-written with a man who didn't have a deal.*

CHAPTER FOUR

Demos

Or, what the heck...just throw your hard earned money down the toilet...

Demos

I really hate writing this chapter...writing this chapter makes me wanna cry. Because this chapter brings me to *A Costly Mistake: Paying too much for my Demos...*

I wish someone would have shaken me. Over that 5 year period before my deal, I must have spent over 3,000 dollars demoing songs that never saw the light of day. That money is gone...fini...bye, bye... it's out of here...

Besides the loss of money, Great Big Demos were a mistake for me for three reasons.

1. If a publisher thought the song still needed work...too bad, the Demo was done.

2. If the publisher liked the song but didn't like the demo...too bad, the Demo was done.

3. Demoing left nothing for the publisher to do... If they really like the song—The Publisher is the one who should make the big Demo.

So what would have been the smart thing to do??

I could have done two things...I could have down sized. Guitar or piano demos would have been more then enough to take to a publisher. OR...I could have invested in my own little home studio. Today it's very affordable and in the long run can save you loads of money.

Now...at the risk of confusing you, there is one part of this process that, for me, was worth dropping a little cash for. I hired real singers and great pickers. I learned quickly that my role in the demo process was to eat donuts and sit in the control room while the professionals made my song shine. It would have been an even greater waste of money if I had my mediocre vocals on those songs.

For those of you reading this Chapter with undeniably great voices...You're in a great position. It's a wonderful thing to be able to sing your own demos. Not only do you save money, but you're also shopping yourself as an artist each time you make a pitch.

All power to you. Rock on! But for those of you like me who can't even sing in the shower...Just admit it! Give your songs what they need to shine. BUT, once again, that doesn't mean you need to spend a ton of money like I did. Musicians and singers would be happy to come over to your home studio.

So to sum up this chapter...

1. Don't over demo! All a publisher needs to hear is a sweet vocal and guitar.

2. If you can sing and play...Excellent! But if you can't, face the truth and meet me at The Krispy Kreme donut shop!

CHAPTER FIVE

Okay...time to start visiting the publishers.

(Pay attention.
This is my favorite chapter.)

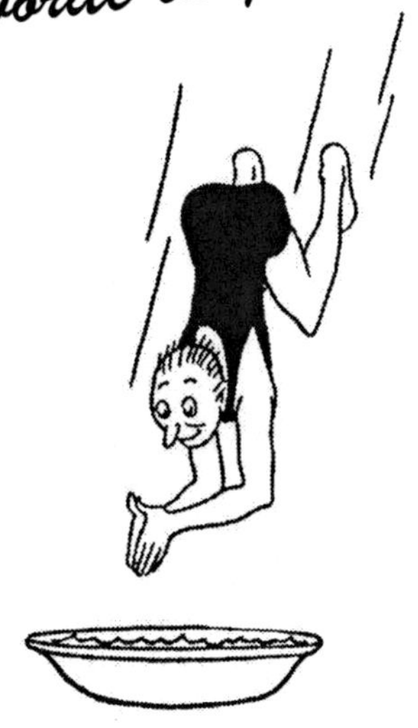

Okay...time to start visiting the publishers.

Ahhhhh, but how do you get in? Can't just call up the assistant and say, "Are you looking for staff writers?" The answer to that question will be "Why? Are they missing??" But seriously folks... The answer is...there's no easy answer. But where there's a will, there's a way.

The first thing I did was to go back to some of the NSAI symposiums. At these events were lots of song pluggers from respected companies in town. The most important thing I got out of this were NAMES. Can't get past that assistant if you don't know the name of the plugger. So at every lecture, I'd sit in the back and scribble the names of these guys on my little pad. Did I get through to these pluggers?? Most of the time...no. But some wonderful voices actually said YES.

I also paid a visit to ASCAP. Their job is to be helpful to songwriters and that they were. They listened to my material and set up a couple of very good appointments for me. I would highly recommend this route, be it ASCAP, BMI or SESAC. These are people who you will be doing business with and you might as well get to know them.

So I got some meetings. With my 3 songs on one tape...(we used tapes back in the cave man days) I marched into the offices of Mr. or Mrs. Important song person. A variety of scenarios happened to me:

1. Some Publishers were not at all impressed with my songs. I didn't get defensive...I just shook their hands and thanked them for the meeting.

2. Some Publishers liked what they heard...but not enough to offer me anything. However, they usually said I was invited back

anytime I had something I was excited about. I definitely took them up on this.

3. Some Publishers liked what they heard and offered me a Single Song Contract for the song.

4. NO publishers offered me a writing deal...not at this point...

This stuff is somewhat important...so let's look at it really close.

Scenario One

In the beginning rejection was something I got very used to... It happened all the time. This stone faced man or woman would turn off my song before it even got to the chorus. What I wanted to say was...*What are you doing??!! This song is great you deaf &%@$#!!! How the @%$&* did you get your job buddy??!!* What I did say was..."Hey, thanks for meeting with me, I appreciate it." Then I was gone. What else could I do? I couldn't insult the guy. This is a very small town. VERY SMALL. If you don't think song pluggers talk to one another, think again! If you're rude to people, the word will get out like wild fire! The rule of thumb is an old one...Don't burn any bridges. The ironic thing about all of it is, in retrospect, these publishers weren't deaf at all. My songs were still weak. I just couldn't see it at the time.

Scenario 2

This was probably the most interesting scenario. They liked me, liked the songs (even to the point of singing along) but just not enough. However, these meeting usually ended with a comment like "Please come by again when you have more songs." It's so important to not take this as rejection. If they say to come by again...do it. They're testing you. They want to see how much you want it. But beware of something. *THE IDEA IS TO BE PROFESSIONAL...*

NOT A PEST. I will cover this in a later chapter...but basically it's a fine line and you must be careful. Calling a publisher 10 times a day is being a pest. Trying to get him twice in one week is being professional.

Scenario 3

This probably kept me from packing up and going back home. Publishers started offering me Single Song Contracts. For those who don't know what a Single Song Contract is, it's a publishing agreement on one song...not on you as a writer. For example if you sign a contract on one of your songs for let's say 2 years, that means that company has that amount of time to try and get your song recorded and released. It's a binding contract in the way that that song cannot be brought to another publisher during that time. But let me stress...This contract is only binding on a song-by-song basis. New songs you write are yours until you sign them over.

Anyway...back to me. Little by little I was offered these contracts on my songs. I signed everyone of them without hesitation. I had to take a chance. Some contracts had reversion clauses in them which meant I'd get the song back in usually 2 years and some contracts signed these songs for life. Either way, I looked at it as just one song. What could I lose?

Scenario 4

THEY WANT MY SONGS BUT THEY DON'T WANT ME! WHY??? This baffled me for a long time because it kept happening. A company would take a song of mine, but when it came to putting me on staff as a writer...Sorry—see ya later. I just couldn't understand why. Now I know why...

I wasn't being consistent. For example I would bring JOE PUBLISHING company a great song. They would sign that great song. Now they're thinking..."OK...what else can she do??" The next week I bring JOE PUBLISHER a mediocre song...now they're disappointed. *They have to see that you have more then one great song in you.* Signing someone as a staff writer is a big deal and it's not taken lightly. If you don't produce...that publisher loses face. If you write great songs he looks good for signing you. To put it plain and simple: *EVERYBODY WANTS TO KEEP THEIR JOB.* If you write a hit, the publisher keeps his job. Then the producer who found your hit keeps his job. And finally when that songs goes to number one... the Artist keeps her job. Am I saying it's all about Money? You bet I am.

At the time I was searching for a staff writing deal, these publishers just didn't think I was a writer who would make them a lot of money. And , looking back, they were right. I still had so much to learn. But still I blamed them and not myself. "They all suck!" I'd spout. In the midst of my complaining...another 2 years went by and I was still a waitress.

So...to sum up this chapter:

1. If you're sure you're ready,
start visiting the publishers.

2. Come in with no more then 5 songs...
3 would be excellent!

3. If they don't like your songs,
don't take it personally.

4. If they invite you back when you have more songs...
TAKE THEM UP ON IT.
And don't wait too long.

5. If they offer you a single song publishing deal...
Sign it. You've got little to lose with one song.
Just make sure you respect the company.

6. If you're not offered a writing deal yet, don't let
it get you down. You may not be ready for one.

CHAPTER SIX

Forget about fair...

I'm so glad I'm GiGi!!!

Forget about fair...

So, let's see...At this point in time I'm really busting my little butt...I'm waking up at 8am to search for a great idea to write with my co-writer...from 10am to 4pm I'm co-writing...from 5pm to 1 in the morning I'm waiting tables at NOODLES...an Italian restaurant that leaves me smelling like a clove of garlic every night. And while I'm doing this the unthinkable happens...Some 20 year old girl who looks like she just stepped out of a Victoria Secret catalogue, comes sailing into town. She's been here less then a month and is offered 3 publishing deals while I'm sitting in my apartment on the phone begging some receptionist to put my call through...THAT'S NOT FAIR !!!

Well that's very true. It's not "Fair". But whoever said that Fair played any part in this at all. Truth is, in any business, the word fair makes little sense. The facts are just the facts. Let's call our little Victoria Secret nightmare GIGI. GIGI can sing...She sings pretty good. The fact that she has never written a song makes no difference.

If Joe Publisher signs GIGI and GIGI lands a deal at let's say Capitol Records, well then...every song GIGI writes will magically appear on the CD...making Joe Publisher able to buy a really big boat...What would you do if you were Joe Publisher???

Before you answer, remember that this is a business and you're trying to keep the lights on. This is not to say that that same publisher wouldn't hire a writer he totally believes is brilliant. The truth is, he or she has to do both.

So I stamped my feet, cried in my pillow, cursed GIGI'S name, and once again got no further in my pursuit as a successful songwriter...

What should I have done??...Well...

1. I should have minded my own business...
Everybody's luck is different. Concentrating on my own career should have been my only concern.

2. I should have been happy for GiGi...
that would have been the right Karmic path...

3. Instead of being mad at GiGi, I should have asked her to co-write...I might have made it on that album that sold a million copies...

CHAPTER SEVEN

I'm tired of this... I'm moving back home!

I'm tired of this... I'm moving back home!

So...at this point Gigi's got a staff writing deal and I don't. I'm about to turn thirty and I'm feeling like I'll be waiting tables forever... Nothing is being offered to me in the way of a deal and I miss home terribly...

So I went home...

For one month I went back and regrouped. I forgot about the music business and just cleared my head. I went to movies, read books, hung out with family and tried to enjoy my life again. It was the best thing I could have done for myself. I didn't realize till then that after 5 years I was in desperate need of a break.

When I returned to Nashville I still wasn't completely ready to start up again. I needed a new game plan. One that incorporated positive thinking. So the first thing I did was to buy self help tapes. You might think it's silly, but they absolutely saved me and changed my perspective.

Leo Buscaglia, Dr. Wayne W. Dyer, and Gerald Jampolsky all spoke about the power of the mind to transform your life.

I joined a church and began embracing God. That power added light and happiness to my life. And I joined a gym to release tensions that have been building up for years.

This was my 5th year in Nashville. I suddenly felt that I had graduated some kind of College and that now more then ever, I was ready. I was right. I now had the right attitude, the right temperament, and the right songs.

Moving home is the right move for many people. I personally have many friends who finally came to grips with the fact that Nashville was not right for them. But if that's not you then...

1.Take a break. If that means leaving for a couple of weeks... do it. When you come back, regroup. Find a path that will keep you positive. This could be through a church or temple, through self-help tapes, or maybe just by working out everyday.

2. Get back to work, but with a better attitude.

CHAPTER EIGHT

The heartbreak of writer's block!

The heartbreak of writer's block!

This was always my excuse for running out to the mall and maxing out my credit card. If I couldn't write then I'd spend money, a really bad thing for my bank account.

The truth is that Writer's Block sent me into a panic. I was sure it meant my creative side had vanished and would never return. This would make everything worse. I'd sit for hours with my guitar to no avail. And then I'd give up...sometimes giving up for weeks on end.

I now can't afford Writer's Block. If I have an important writing appointment—good mood or bad mood...I've got to try my best. If I don't try my best, I won't get that appointment again. My motivation is simple...my PAYCHECK.

But how do you try your best when you're blocked??? Simple... if the muse doesn't come naturally...go to the muse. The muse can be found in books, movies, records, even TV shows.* All you need is a pad and pencil close by at all times. Or if you're like me, the back of junk mail always works great. See for yourself. Go to a movie sometime in Nashville. When Tom Cruise says to Rene Zellweger "You had me at Hello"...just see how many writers start scribbling in the dark.

What I'm saying is that you need to keep the well filled. If you're not feeling inspired, then find things that will fill your mind with inspiration. It's all a part of doing your homework. Just as dancers practice everyday and doctors constantly read journals, songwriters need to keep their minds nourished.

Another way to unblock yourself is to clear clutter out of your life. Clutter meaning, an unorganized house, unpaid bills, an unresolved fight with a friend...anything filling your brain with junk. If you're like me, it's impossible to be at the top of your game when you've got too much unfinished business in your world.

Sounds like I've got writers block all figured out folks...right??? Wrong. I still get it all the time. But this time I don't go straight to the mall...I go to the book store...

So in summary:

1. Don't panic when you feel blocked...
It happens to every writer.

2. Fill your life with Inspiration. Movies and books are a great way to get song ideas.

**my first cut was inspired by a Charlie Brown comic*

CHAPTER NINE

Choosing your co-writers...

The co-writer from Hell!!

Choosing your co-writers...

In an effort to make it as a big time songwriter, I took a lot of writing appointments. This was absolutely the right thing to do because the more you work the better your chances. And from time to time I wrote with my close friends. I figured the closer you are, the better the songs. Right?? Not necessarily.

The mystery of what makes a good writing partnership is still a head-scatcher to me. I have steady people that I work with now and I absolutely swear by them. They light up my week. For the 4 or 5 hours we spend together...I feel like I could tell them anything. And the songs we write are amazing. But in some cases, that's the end of it. We don't socialize outside of work.

These are the writers I cling to. Nine times out of ten we'll write a song I'm proud to be a part of. For what ever reason they'll bring something out in me that another writer couldn't. I'll feel relaxed enough to let my mind be free. And I'll do the same for them. Simply put...It works.

My biggest challenge is saying NO to relationships that don't work. It's a hard thing to do because feelings get hurt. But this is a business and your time is like gold. You want your book to be filled with people that inspire you and sometimes that's just not your buddy next door.

Sometimes the puzzle doesn't fit with a hit songwriter. During my career I've had appointments with writers that I've admired for years and though some went really well, some turned into the co-write from Hell! And I would always end up beating myself up for it, thinking I'm obviously to blame. I should have come to the table with a better idea...I should have been sharper.

NUTS TO THAT!!… It's either a fit or it's not.

So…

1. When you find a writer you like working with…
Book lots of time together.
You're probably sitting on a hit!

2. Learn to say no when it's not working.
Treat this like a business.

3. Don't beat yourself up when you can't make
the appointment work.
Sometimes that's just the way it goes.

CHAPTER TEN

They want me! (But do I want them?)

They want me! (But do I want them?)

In July of 1990 I had my first meeting with Starstruck Writers group, the publisher who ultimately signed me to my deal. He didn't like anything I brought him. However, he did say to come back anytime. I came back the next week. Once again, he didn't take anything. Two weeks later I asked for another meeting. This time he liked one song and offered me a single song contract on it. This began our 9-month dance together. No deal offered for me as a writer, just single song contracts on songs he liked. But something told me to stay with this company and not to give up. I wanted to show them how much I wanted it. Finally in April 1991, they offered me a staff writing deal. I thought I had died and gone to heaven.

But still I was careful. I took the contract they offered me right to a lawyer. Except for a couple of snags, it was fine. And then I talked to the writers that were on staff already. Some were positive about the company, some were negative. I just had to use my own judgment. I also quizzed higher ups on Music Row like BMI and ASCAP. Luckily they all said this was a good place to sign. And sign I did. Six months later I was celebrating my first cut, first single and my first number one song "For My Broken Heart" with Reba McEntire. Without taking away my talent as a writer, I have to say that this was a real live case of beginners luck. Most people who sign publishing deals don't see their first cut for awhile. For me though, I guess at that time the stars were in the right place. Or perhaps the angels thought that 5 years of waiting tables was enough for me.

It's so important not to get carried away when you're offered a deal. You must investigate the company and then make your decision. If they don't have a good reputation on Music Row, you don't want to be with them. No deal is better then a bad deal. The last thing you want is to be locked in an awful place.

So here's what to do when you're offered a staff writing deal:

1. Ask yourself, is this a company I want to be with. Do they get many cuts.?? Do they have enough money to stay in business??

2. Find out how happy the writers are at that company.

3. Do you like the song pluggers?? Do they have a good reputation??

4. Go directly to a music lawyer and make sure the contract is okay. Once you're sure you want to be there, sign away!

CHAPTER ELEVEN

How much money should I ask for?

How much money should I ask for?

When I signed my writing deal in the spring of 1991 I was paid a draw of only 100 dollars per week. Before I go any further let me explain a draw…

A draw is not a real salary. A draw is a weekly advance against future royalties. So, for instance, if you're paid let's say 100 dollars per week, that money goes on a statement that you receive twice a year. If you have not received any royalties at the end of the year, then you would be in the "RED" to your company for about 5000 dollars. If you have received royalties then there's a good chance you'd be in the BLACK… meaning your publisher owes you money.

If a writer takes a high draw from his publisher but doesn't get any songs recorded at the end of his contract, he runs the risk of losing his deal. He will have fallen too far into the Red. No matter how much that publisher may believe in him, he might have to let him go. Once released from contract, the writer isn't required to repay the "draw" monies, but...it's back to the street.

My reasons for taking such a low draw back then were simple. I wanted to keep my job and take the pressure off myself. At 100 dollars per week, I was not a high risk for any company. This lack of pressure made me more creative. True, I was still serving Pigs knuckles at the German restaurant 4 nights a week—but the struggle just inspired me to write. When more of my songs started getting recorded, my deal was renegotiated so I could quit the restaurant business. However, like it still is today, my draw was pretty modest.

Once again, every story is different. I was a single woman without any kids. I didn't need much money to get by. But if you come here and you need to support your family, well then, it's a totally different game. However, from the school I come from, I say...

When you're first starting out, don't ask for the world. Get your cuts and then you can redo your contract.

Also...

I would highly advise you to get educated on the different kinds of deals and contracts you can sign. NSAI has a book store where they carry several books on this topic.

CHAPTER TWELVE

I got a writing deal!! The hard part is over, right??

I got a writing deal!! The hard part is over, right??

Nope. This is where the hard part begins. When you're a new writer you're in the position of having to prove yourself and that can be a lot of pressure. The publishers are watching you very closely this first year. They want to see how much you're writing and who you're writing with. They want to see how much action they get on your songs. They want to make sure you want it bad. I hated this first year. But everyone goes through it and once you get your first cut, it's a bit easier. You just have to work really hard.

Now is not the time to be lazy. In other words...*SHOW UP FOR WORK!* This is something I should have glued to my mirror every morning because by nature I love staying in bed and watching CNN all day (news junkie). But look at it this way...every writing appointment has the potential of being a 200,000 dollar day. What if the writers of "I Hope You Dance" decided to cancel each other that day and rearrange their sock drawer instead...Am I making myself clear??? Don't worry if you feel uninspired. Don't worry if you never met the co-writer and you're nervous. Show up and see what happens. In truth, I almost canceled the writing appointment that lead to my first cut and my first #1. I didn't really know him very well and I was just not up to it. Thank God I went. I might still be serving Pigs' Knuckles at the German Restaurant.

Another way to show up for work is to shop your songs around town. Call the A&R folks at the record companies and say "This is Joe Smith, I work for Big Time Publishing. Can I play you my new demo session??" If they say to drop it off, do it. If they say to come by, get over there. You have a calling card now. You're with a major Publishing company and now you have some credibility. Just be sure to let your publisher know what you're doing. If they don't mind your helping them out, don't hesitate. This is something I've done from the beginning of my professional career and it's gotten me several cuts. It's also gives you a clue as to how tough it is out there, and how good your songs have to be to measure up.

But how do you get these appointments??? How do you know who runs these A&R departments??? Well there's this amazing invention you all should know about. It's a secret of mine, so keep it under wraps. Are you ready?? Okay…It's called…THE PHONE!!! Once you pick it up you'll be amazed at the information you can get. Writers always ask me how I get my meetings. It's simple. I make a call and I ask. Maybe it's the Brooklyn in me, but I've never understood why that's such a difficult concept to understand.

Writing songs for a living is an honor. It's a wonderful way to make a living. You're a staff writer and so many never get that far. It's really wonderful to be paid for being creative. Some call staff writing a mill...that it's not artistic. I don't buy that. I like the discipline of having to turn in songs. It helps me.

How to keep your deal?? Well that's a whole other book. I'm still working hard at keeping mine. In the slow years I believe having a low draw helped me. It gave me a chance to get my steam back.

So the 2 important things to remember when you get signed is...

1. Show up! A plumber shows up,
the cable guy shows up…*
You have to show up.

2. Enjoy yourself...it's a great way to make a living.

**Actually, sometimes the cable guy doesn't show up….*

Part 2:

Nashville Etiquette

Making it as a Nashville songwriter
doesn't necessarily make you any wiser.
I find myself always needing a reminder
of how to conduct myself out there in
the songwriting world.

This part of my book is for the
wanna be writer and the successful writer...
Just a set of rules to live by in Nashville...
Here goes...

Being a pest vs. being a professional.

1. Calling a publishing company 10 times a day is being Pest! Checking in with a publishing company maybe twice a month is being professional.

2. Disturbing a publisher or producer at a restaurant when they are trying to relax is being a pest! Letting that producer or publisher eat in peace is being professional.

3. Cornering an established writer you don't know and asking them to co-write is being a pest. Getting to know that person over time is being professional.

4. Arguing with a publisher when they turn off your song is being a pest. Handling rejection is being professional.

5. Talking about yourself constantly is being a pest. Listening and learning is being professional.

6. Putting down the music business to everyone you meet is being a pest. Staying positive is being professional.

As I mentioned earlier, Nashville is a very small town and people talk. Please don't develop a bad reputation. It will take years to live it down. No matter what level you're at, remember to do business like a pro.

There have always been these unwritten rules for co-writing in Nashville. However I think it's about time someone spelled them out.

1. When you enter a room with someone and start working on a song, the share is 50/50 all the way. No counting lines, no complaining that the other writer didn't do enough on it. None of that stupid stuff. 50/50...end of story.

2. If you've started a song with a writer and you'd like to bring in another writer to help it along, only do so with the other writer's permission. It's just plain rude not to.

3. Be flexible during a writing appointment. If your co-writer is passionate that something is wrong or right, hear them out. It's all for the good of the song.

4. If you bring an idea to a writer and begin a song...it's now a Co-write. Taking back the idea and writing it with another writer is wrong unless you've cleared it with the original writer.

5. Don't demo a song unless you are both in agreement that the song is done. If your writer feels it needs to be looked at one more time, maybe it does.

6. Treat each other with respect and be open minded. The idea is to become a writer who's enjoyable to be with. The last thing anyone needs is a reputation for being difficult. If you do you won't get many people coming back for another appointment.

Just remember to enjoy yourself and to act like a writer you'd want to be around.

Part 3:

What do I do if I can't move to Nashville???

Some Suggestions.

Here are my suggestions. Remember that I'm not talking from experience...I've lived here for over 20 years.

However, if I were you, this is what I'd do.

1. First of all make sure you always stay a member of NSAI. Their song seminars and song camps are vital for your Nashville education.

2. Try to attend every Publisher Night that they have. I can't think of a better way to get your foot in the door. Call NSAI and mark all of them on your calendar. Publisher nights happen in Nashville... not your home town. It would be a good excuse for a trip.

***3. Come here as often as possible.
For the serious songwriter...6 times a year...
For the VERY SERIOUS songwriter...
Once a month!***

4. When you first come here, you don't necessarily need to visit the publishers right away. Instead, get a feel for how the town works. Attend seminars at NSAI, go to showcases at the Bluebird Café, hit the open Mic's and meet songwriters. In the beginning... Relax and have a good time. Don't be desperate.

5. Visit ASCAP, BMI and SESAC. If they think you're ready, they'll hook you up with writers and publishers. If not...still keep meeting with them. They can be your sounding board for awhile.

6. Once you start your search for a Publishing company that might be interested in signing you—be professional. Enter their office with 5 songs you feel strongly about. NO MORE THAN THAT! Less is always more. Have your songs ready on the CD (don't make them search) and type up your lyrics—this is a job interview.

7. In my opinion… your goal should be to find that ONE great publisher who really digs your songs. Whether they sign you to a staff deal is not important in the beginning. What is important is that you have a contact… someone to send your music to. Having a representative in Nashville will take some of the pressure off your shoulders when not living here.

8. Finding that ONE great publisher could take you 2 months…or 5 years—don't worry about it. Everyone's luck is different. If you really want this, just keep making your trips and learning the business.

9. HERE'S THE REALITY CHECK….The chances of finding success in this business without making frequent trips to Nashville are almost impossible. It's the difference between a Pipe dream and a Real dream. Pipe dreams are fantasies. Real Dreams come true—and they come true because you've earned them.

In Summary

So here it is guys...everything we talked about in a nut shell. Turn to this list when you just need a bit of a boost to keep you going.

1. If you've just arrived to Nashville, calm down.
Give yourself a chance to see how it works.

2. Don't hang out with negative songwriters.
They will bring you way down.

3. Make sure your job doesn't take you away
from your goal as a staff writer.

4. Keep your radio tuned to the country station.
Stay current.

5. Go to shows at the Bluebird cafe.
Let the talent inspire you.

6. Don't over demo.

7. Start treating yourself like you're already
a staff writer. Write everyday.

8. Learn to handle rejection.
That's 80% of this business.

*9. If a publisher says to come back again, do it.
Show him you're hungry.*

10. Keep in mind that EVERYONE WANTS TO KEEP THEIR JOB! Are your songs good enough to make that publisher keep his job?

11. Do whatever it takes for you to stay positive.

12. Don't be ashamed if you feel jealous of other writers who are more successful than you. Just channel all that energy into writing great songs.

13. Don't panic when you get writer's block. Just find things to fill your mind with inspiration.

14. If offered a staff writing deal, make sure you want to be there. And don't even think about not seeing a lawyer.

*15. If you sign with a company, work hard.
Show them they made a wise decision.*

*16. Be someone that's easy to work with.
Respect your co-writers.*

*17. Enjoy yourself...even enjoy the struggle.
You're trying to make a dream come true.*

That takes a lot of courage.

One more very important thing...

I began writing this book 2 years ago in my off time. Since then it's amazing how much the business has changed.

The advent of illegal downloading of our music has had a catastrophic effect on the entire business. Songwriters, musicians, studio owners, publishers and anyone connected to the industry are in jeopardy of losing their jobs. Last month alone over 200 million files were illegally downloaded from Peer to Peer services. I personally know several songwriters who have been forced out of the business because publishing companies just can't afford to keep them on.

There is a dangerous mind set out there that feels that music should be "For The People." And therefore should be free. I'm just wondering if they feel that half of their paycheck should be "For The People" as well.

Getting music over the computer is here to stay. I personally love it and think it can be great for writers. We just need to be paid.. When done illegally it's Shoplifting. Unless you own the copyright, it's not yours to distribute. Please send the message out to your friends and family and if you're currently in College, let your dorm buddies know.

This is your future...Unless we fight for our right to be paid, we won't be.

And if we're not, the American songwriter will cease to exist.

Handy Information

Handy information

Four major Publishers in Town
(there are hundreds... but here's a start):

SONY PUBLISHING 615-726-8300
EMI PUBLISHING 615-742-8081
WARNER CHAPPELL 615-733-1880
UNIVERSAL PUBLISHING 615-340-9331

My Favorite Demo Studios:

County Q 615-298-1434
Tombstone 615-292-9028

The Performing Rights Organizations:

ASCAP 615-742-5000
BMI 615-401-2000
SESAC 615-320-0055

My favorite Clubs in town for
writers nights and Open Mic's:

The Bluebird Café 615-383-1461
Douglas Corner Café 615-298-1688
Hotel Preston 615-361-5900

About the author

Liz Hengber has had four number one songs recorded by Reba McEntire and hit singles with Andy Griggs, Clay Davidson, Trick Pony and Peter Cetera. She's also had songs recorded by Conway Twitty, Deana Carter, Rick Trovino, Vince Gill, Bombshell, Trace Adkins, Lisa Brokop, Julie Roberts, Lee Greenwood, Lari White, Linda Davis, Jennifer Day, Trent Willmon, James Otto and Lila McCann.

She is a proud board member for the *Nashville Songwriters Association International* and the mother of Wally, the best golden retriever in the world and Sofia...the Cat who, for the time being, lets Liz reside in her home.

Printed in the United States
118501LV00004B/46-57/A

9 781583 851074